How to Explain AEROSPACE ENGINEERING to a Grown-Up

RUTH SPIRO

Illustrated by TERESA MARTÍNEZ

Charlesbridge

When I was a little kid,

I asked a LOT of questions:

Why do some people wear glasses?

Where do fossils come from?

I thought my grown-up had all the answers.

But now that I'm big, I know the truth.
MY GROWN-UP DOES NOT KNOW ALL THE ANSWERS!
Sometimes they need ME to explain things to THEM.
If you're reading this, I'm guessing YOUR grown-up needs help understanding stuff, too.

With a little help from this book,
YOU can explain AEROSPACE ENGINEERING to your grown-up!

First, show your grown-up this book.

They may ask,

It looks like you have a LOT of explaining to do.
Start with something simple, like . . .

that bird.

Your grown-up already knows it can fly, which is a good place to start.

Quietly observe the bird together. You'll notice it doesn't just float up into the sky.

Gravity

Pro Tip

Making real-life connections to something familiar is a perfect way to begin learning something new.

Why? Gravity is pulling the bird down to Earth.
A push or pull, like gravity, is called a force.

Luckily for the bird, there's also an opposite force, called lift. How does the bird use lift to fly?

With its wings, of course!

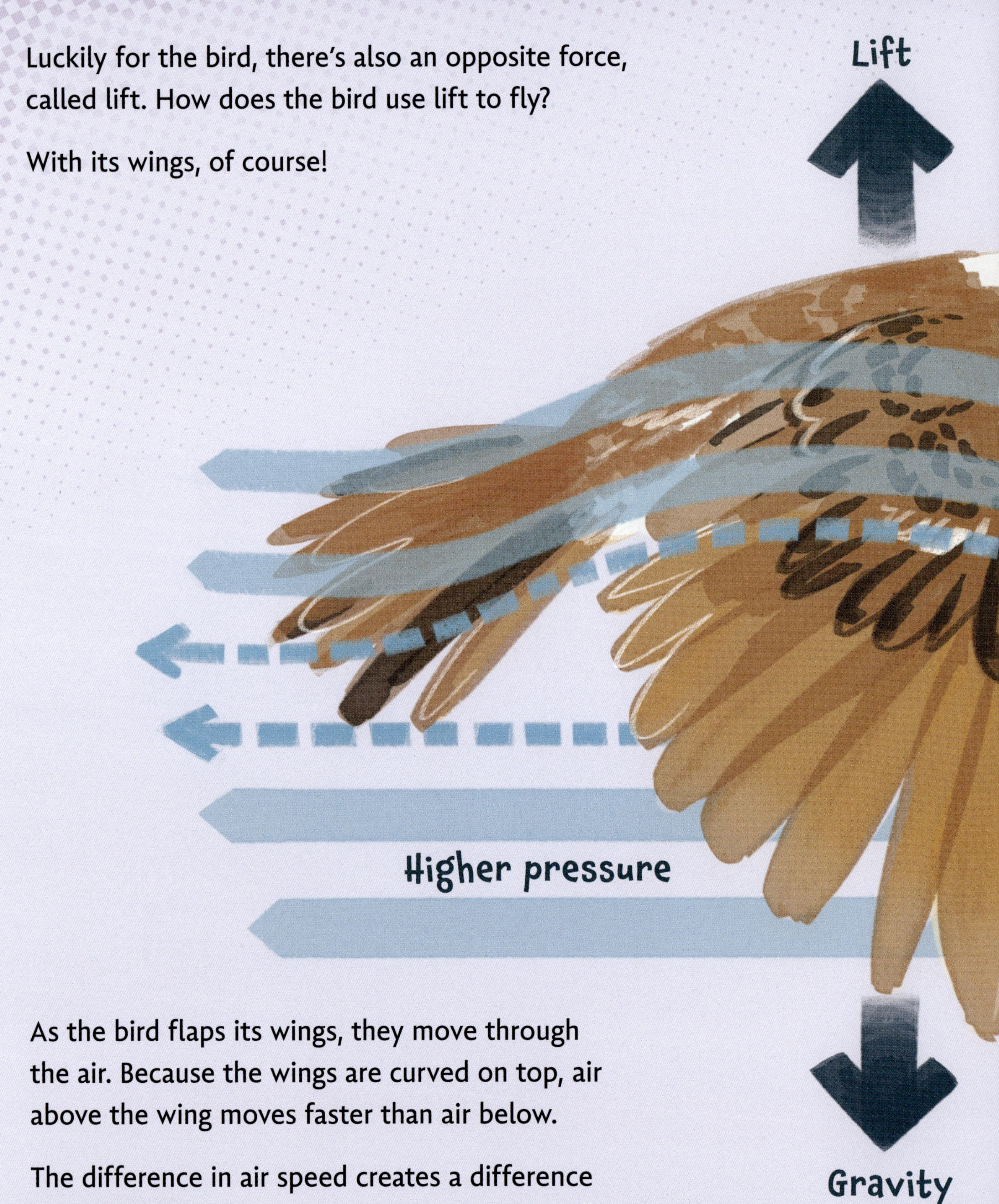

As the bird flaps its wings, they move through the air. Because the wings are curved on top, air above the wing moves faster than air below.

The difference in air speed creates a difference in air pressure.

This difference in air pressure causes lift, and . . .

Lift helps the bird fly!

The science of how things like birds and airplanes move through the air is called aerodynamics. Of course, there are big differences between a bird and an airplane.

For one, an airplane doesn't hatch from an egg. Someone has to build it. Aeronautical engineers design airplanes and other machines that fly.

How else is an airplane different from a bird?

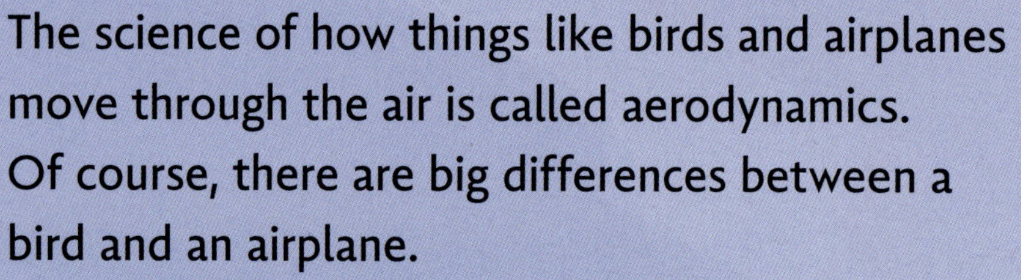

These are all excellent answers!
But there's one more that's very important.
Pro Tip
It's okay if your grown-up needs a hint!
Does an airplane flap its wings?

An airplane can't move by itself. It needs engines.

An engine sucks in air, which includes oxygen. It combines the air with fuel and compresses the mixture. Then it lights the mixture with a spark, causing the oxygen to burn.

The burning gas expands and bursts from the back of the engine, pushing the plane forward. This pushing force is called thrust.

The opposite force that pulls back on the airplane is called drag. When thrust is greater than drag, the airplane moves forward.

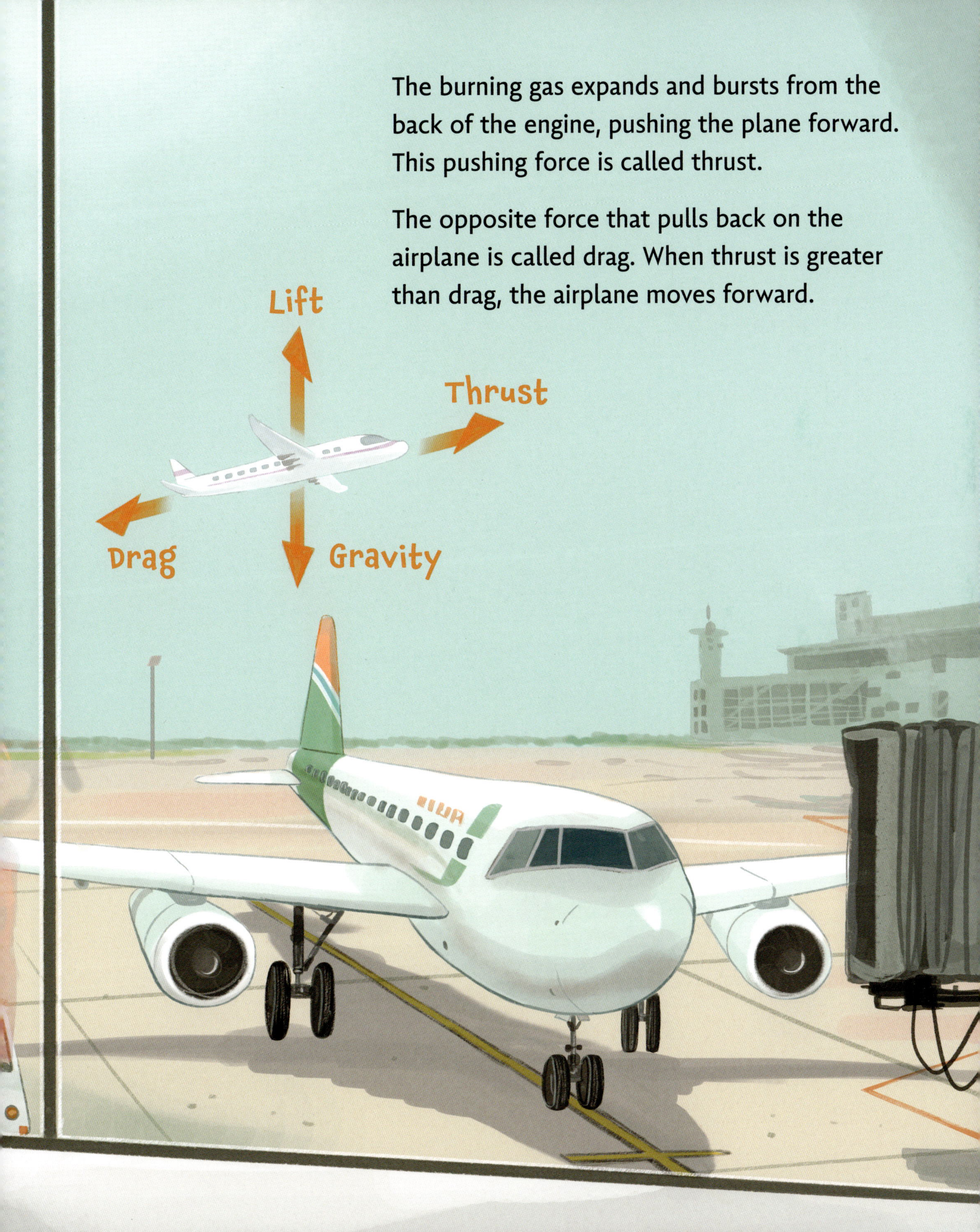

The engines move the airplane forward, but they don't lift it. That's the job of the wings.

As the airplane speeds down the runway, air rushes over its wings. The air above the wing moves faster than the air below, creating a difference in air pressure and lifting the airplane.

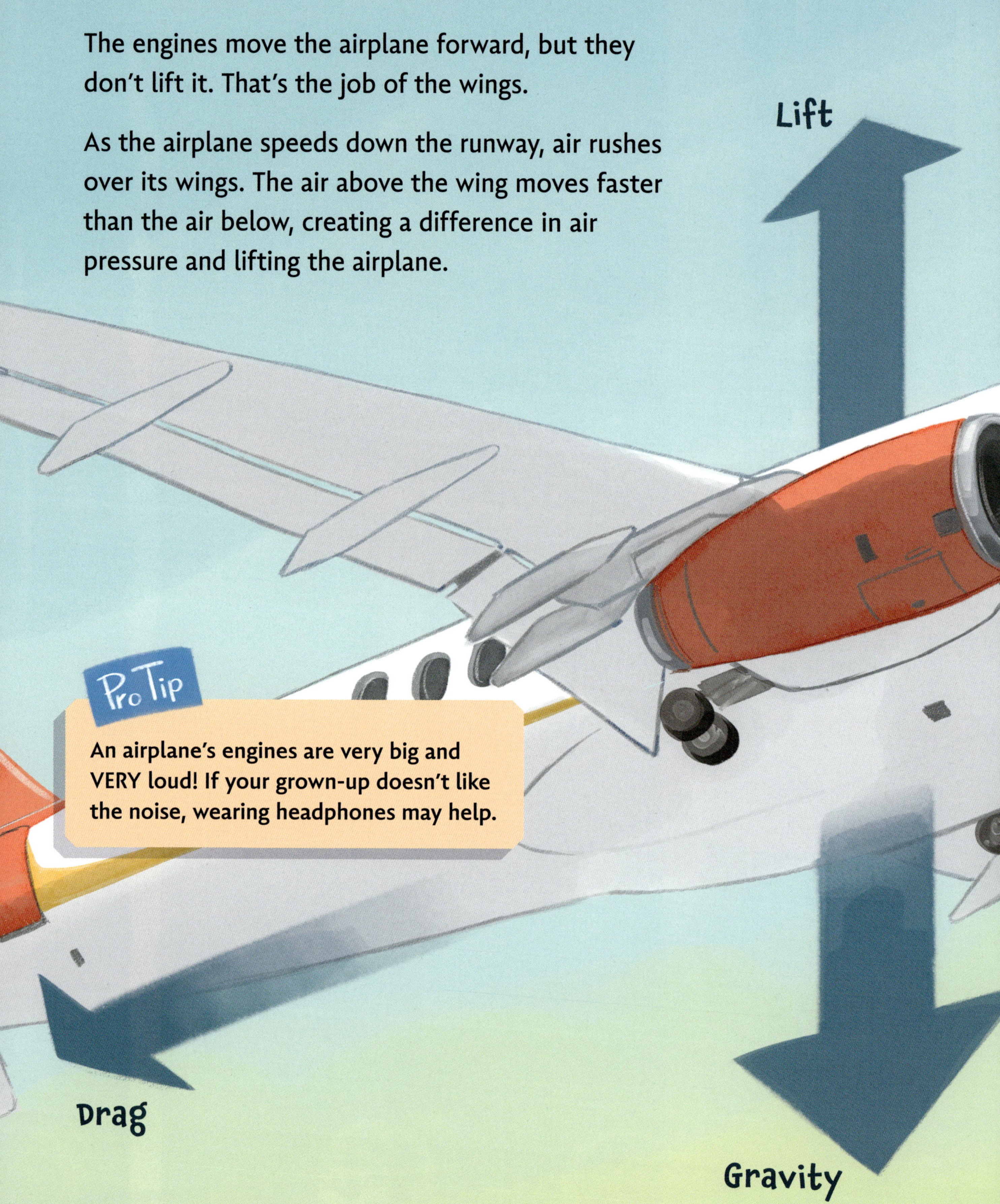

Pro Tip

An airplane's engines are very big and VERY loud! If your grown-up doesn't like the noise, wearing headphones may help.

Airplane wings are "fixed," meaning they don't move. But they have slats and flaps that can be opened or closed to change the airflow.

The airplane has many parts and controls. Someone has to adjust them for takeoff and landing, and in flight.

If your grown-up guessed it's the job of the pilots, they're correct!

Pilots sit at the front of the airplane in the flight deck, or cockpit. They control the airplane and all the systems that make it fly.

Pro Tip
The next time you fly on a plane, make sure to thank the pilots and crew!

Airplanes and other vehicles that fly through the air are called aircraft.

Aircraft can't fly in space. Birds can't fly in space either.

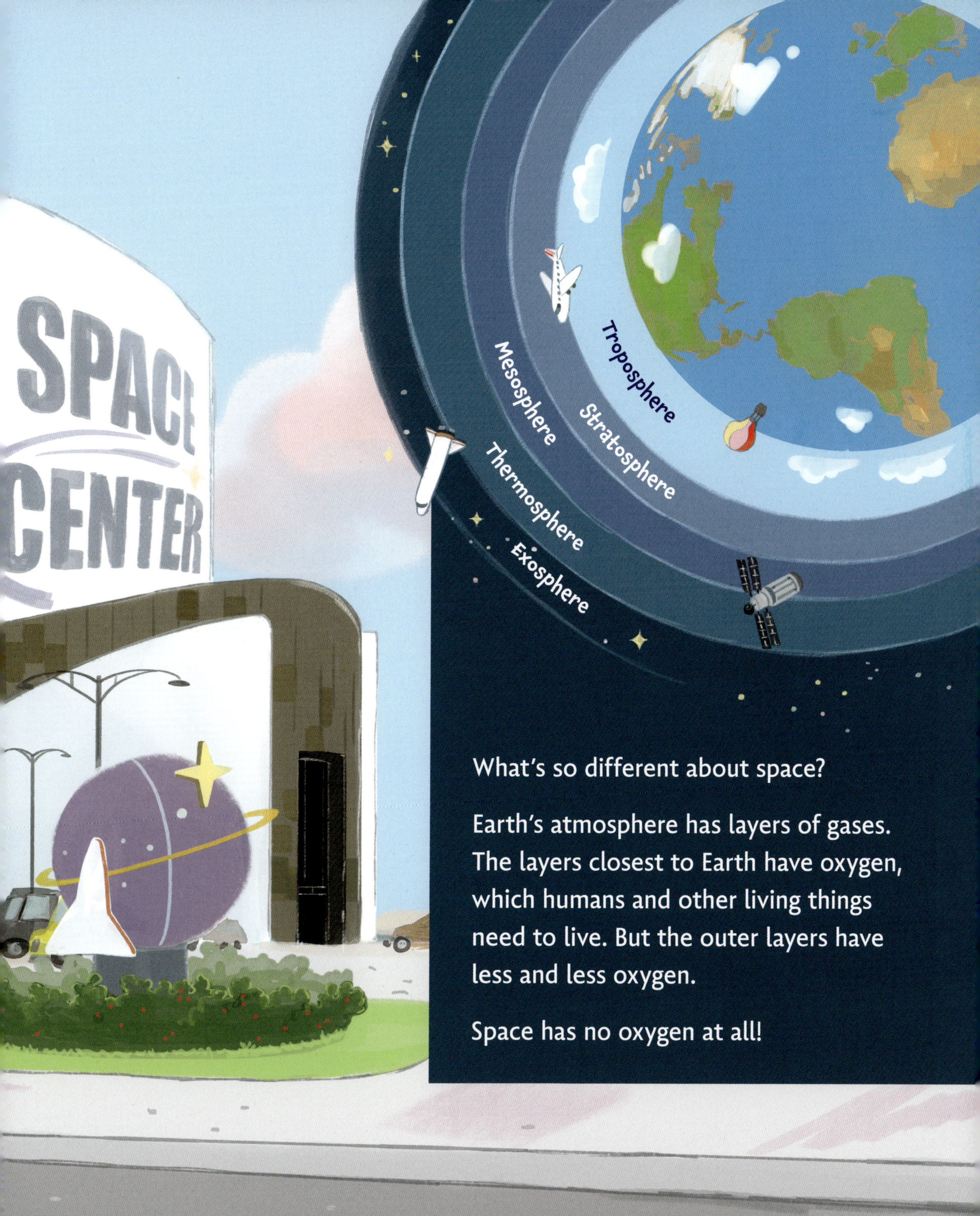

What's so different about space?

Earth's atmosphere has layers of gases. The layers closest to Earth have oxygen, which humans and other living things need to live. But the outer layers have less and less oxygen.

Space has no oxygen at all!

Traveling to space means going beyond Earth's atmosphere, and that requires a spacecraft. Like aircraft, spacecraft need engines to make them move. But aircraft engines won't work for spacecraft because there's no oxygen in space.

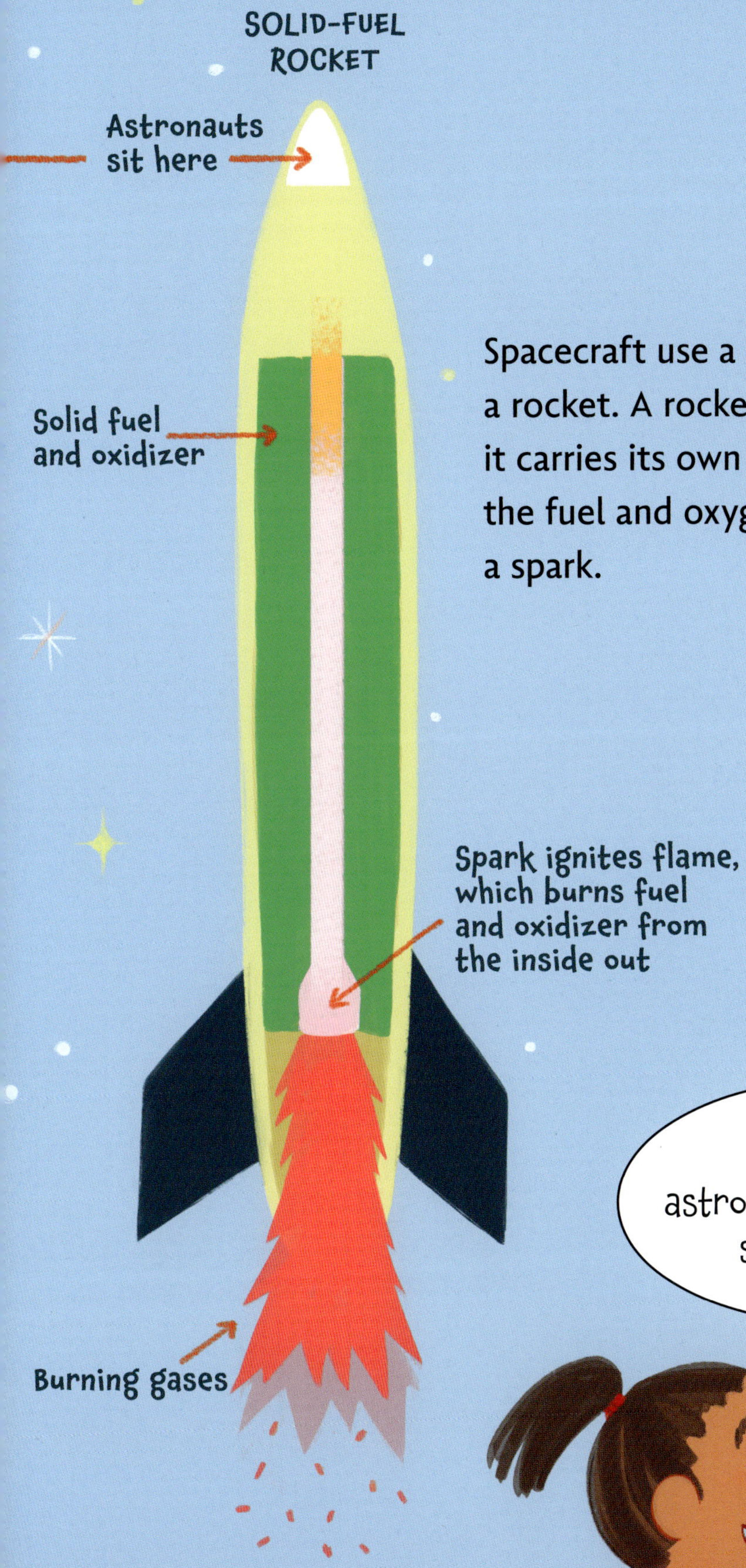

SOLID-FUEL ROCKET

Astronauts sit here

Solid fuel and oxidizer

Spacecraft use a different kind of engine: a rocket. A rocket works in space because it carries its own supply of oxygen. It mixes the fuel and oxygen and lights them with a spark.

Spark ignites flame, which burns fuel and oxidizer from the inside out

Burning gases

Where do astronauts keep their sandwiches?

In a launch box!

The burning gas shoots out of the rocket. The force is so huge that it propels the spacecraft straight up, overcoming Earth's gravity.

People can hear the sound and feel the vibrations from miles away.

As the spacecraft flies higher and higher, the rocket continues to provide thrust, pushing the spacecraft beyond Earth's atmosphere and gravity.

Goodbye, astronauts!

Exploring space is exciting—and not just for astronauts.

Aerospace engineers study and design both aircraft and spacecraft. They solve problems and invent new technology to make each mission safe and efficient.

Your grown-up may be interested to know that many things we use every day come from inventions first used in space!

You've explained a LOT about aerospace engineering to your grown-up!

Now may be a good time to review:

- Aerodynamics is the science of how things like birds and aircraft move through the air.
- Aeronautical engineering is the study and design of airplanes and other vehicles that fly within Earth's atmosphere.
- Aerospace engineering is the study and design of aircraft and spacecraft.

Pro Tip
After learning a lot of new information, reviewing can help your grown-up remember everything better.

Congratulations!

YOU DID IT!
You explained aerospace engineering to a grown-up!
Get ready, because now your grown-up
is going to have a LOT more questions.

Why do we need bees?

What makes a volcano erupt?

What will you explain next?

Space is a busy place!

Aerospace engineers design spacecraft for many different purposes.

Space probes travel through deep space and send information back to scientists on Earth. Someday space probes could be powered by solar sails, which use the force from the sun's rays just like a sailboat uses wind.

Space telescopes help us learn about how stars are born and die, or look for planets that may be like ours.

Crewed spacecraft take astronauts to space stations, the moon, and beyond!

Satellites are used for technology like television, internet, GPS, and weather forecasting.

Space stations allow astronauts to live in space for longer periods of time.

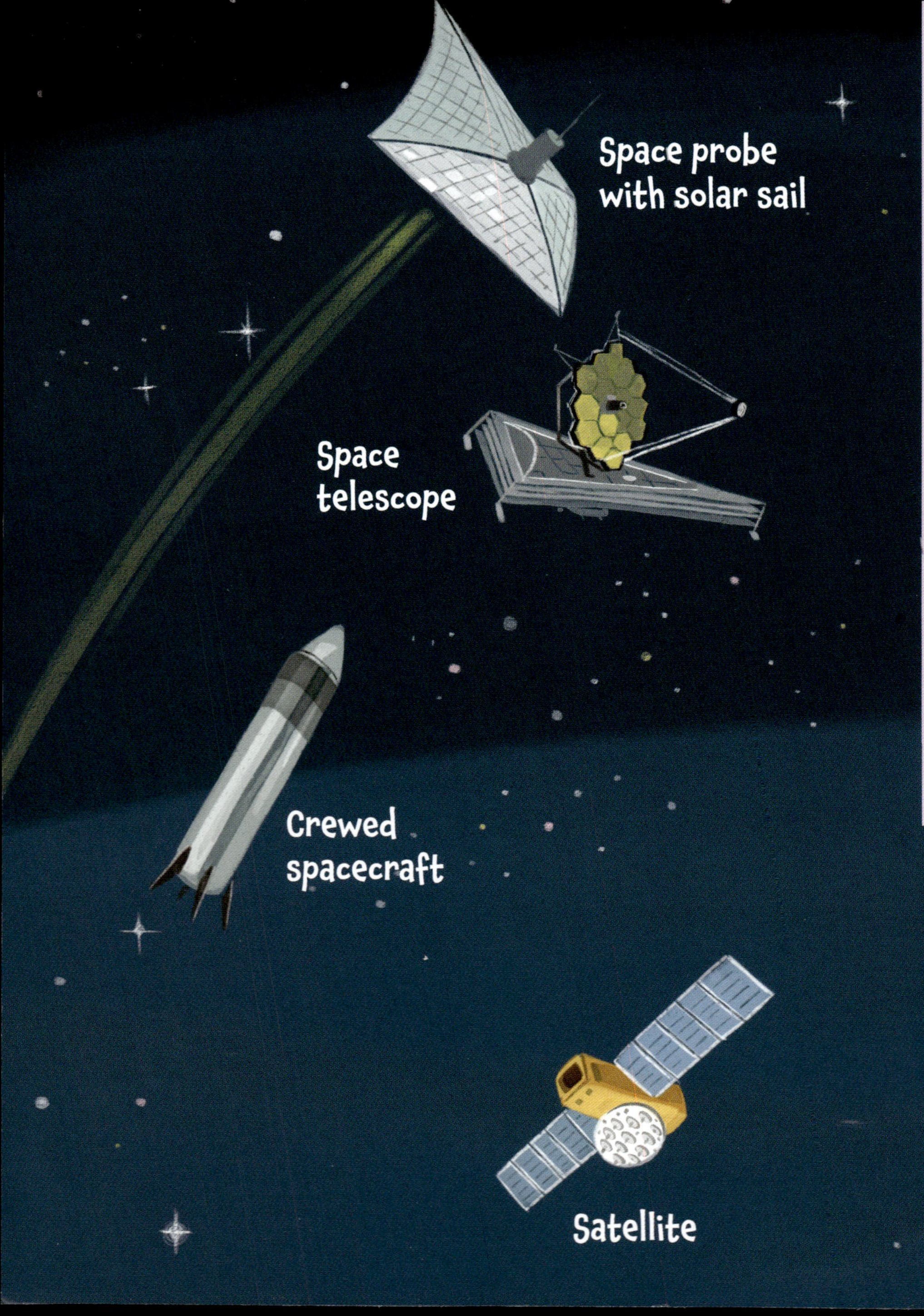

Space probe with solar sail

Space telescope

Crewed spacecraft

Satellite

Space station

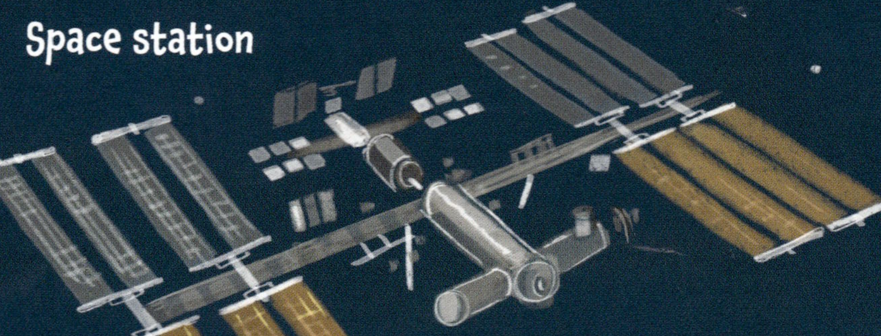

Glossary

aerodynamics: The science of how objects move through the air.

aeronautics: The science of flight within Earth's atmosphere.

aerospace: The science of flight both within Earth's atmosphere and in space.

drag: A force that pulls an object to keep it from moving. Drag is the opposite of thrust.

engine: A machine that turns fuel into energy to make something move.

force: A push or pull on an object.

gravity: A force that pulls objects toward each other.

lift: A force that pushes an object upward.

rocket: A special kind of engine that works in space because it carries its own supply of oxygen.

spacecraft: A vehicle that can fly beyond Earth's atmosphere into space.

thrust: A force that pushes an object to make it move. Thrust is the opposite of drag.

Size and distance of objects are not to scale.

For Bee, Deborah, Rachel, Andrea, Sandy, and the many other remarkable women working to inspire the next generation of STEM innovators and leaders—R. S.

To Kristina, scientist, diver, adventurer, and on top of it all, a darn good pilot—T. M.

Very special thanks to Bee Hayes-Thakore, board director at The Planetary Society, for sharing her invaluable expertise and advice.

Charlesbridge • 9 Galen Street, Watertown, MA 02472
www.charlesbridge.com

Printed in China • OPIC
The authorized representative in the EU for product safety and compliance is eucomply OÜPärnu mnt 139b-14, 11317 Tallinn, Estonia, hello@eucompliancepartner.com, +33757690241
(hc) 10 9 8 7 6 5 4 3 2 1

Illustrations created digitally using Photoshop and a Wacom tablet
Text type set in Fontanella by Guisela Mendoza
Edited by Alyssa Mito Pusey
Designed by Cathleen Schaad
Production supervised by Mira Kennedy

Library of Congress Cataloging-in-Publication Data
Names: Spiro, Ruth author | Martínez, Teresa, 1980– illustrator
Title: How to explain aerospace engineering to a grown-up / Ruth Spiro; illustrated by Teresa Martínez.
Description: Watertown, MA: Charlesbridge, [2026] | Series: How to explain science to a grown-up | Audience: Ages 4–8 | Audience: Grades 2–3 | Summary: "In this tongue-in-cheek guide, an in-the-know narrator instructs the reader in the art of explaining aerospace engineering to a grown-up. Includes information about how birds, airplanes, and spacecraft fly."—Provided by publisher.
Identifiers: LCCN 2024058943 (print) | LCCN 2024058944 (ebook) | ISBN 9781623546212 hardcover | ISBN 9781632892669 ebook
Subjects: LCSH: Aerospace engineering
Classification: LCC TL793 .S6898 2026 (print) | LCC TL793 (ebook) | DDC 629.1—dc23/eng/20250618
LC record available at https://lccn.loc.gov/2024058943
LC ebook record available at https://lccn.loc.gov/2024058944